The Book
of How

British Library Cataloguing-in-Publication Data
A catalogue record for this book is available from
the British Library

ISBN 13: 978-0-8109-9142-6

Copyright © 2005 Editions de la Martinière, Paris
Originally published in French as *Le livre des comment*
by Editions de la Martinière

English translation copyright © 2007 Harry N. Abrams, Inc.
Typesetting for the English edition: Emmanuelle Lallemand

Printed and bound in France
10 9 8 7 6 5 4 3 2 1

HNA
harry n. abrams, inc.
a subsidiary of La Martinière Groupe

The Book of How

Martine Laffon
Hortense de Chabaneix

Illustrations by
Jacques Azam

ABRAMS BOOKS FOR YOUNG READERS

Table of contents

When will I be a grown-up?

When I'm a grown-up,
I can do as I please!
The need to be independent
and make your own decisions
can be so great as you grow older
that you'd do almost anything to enter
the world of adults. But at what
point in life are you considered
a grown-up? Is it merely a
question of age?

In the past,
certain cultural rites
of passage marked
the end of adolescence
and the initiation
to adulthood. Young people
slowly let go of their
childhood through a series
of important, life-changing
events. The status of being
a 'child' comes to an end,
but is reborn under
a different guise.

In traditional cultures,
such as in Africa, young people
must prove their courage,
responsibility, strength and respect for
the values of the community, before
they can be considered an adult.

The age at which
children enter adulthood
has varied over the years,
depending on the time period
and the country of origin. Nowadays,
in the United Kingdom, the passage
to adulthood occurs at eighteen:
at this age, a person can vote
and participate in society
as a legal citizen.

But becoming
a grown-up is not simply
a matter of turning a certain
age. You also have to act
the part of an adult by behaving
yourself and not acting out or
foolishly following a whim.
The qualities and values imposed
on and acquired by children
throughout their lives are the keys
to becoming an adult. But this
doesn't happen overnight!
After all, in life, you never
really stop growing…

How do I catch a cold?

A long time ago, people thought that being exposed to cold weather could result in a cold. Thankfully, our bodies aren't that fragile. Nevertheless, during colder months, we stay inside more, making it easier to spread viruses from one person to another.

'I'm the cold virus!'

First I'll cause a little nasal swelling...

then I'll hit the bronchial tubes!' Attack!

The most common cold virus is from the rhinovirus family. This virus makes itself at home in the nasal cavity, causing inflammation, which results in runny noses and sneezing. These viruses are spread through the air, and are very contagious.

Each time you cough or yawn without covering your mouth, lay your handkerchief around carelessly or spit, you run the risk of contaminating the people around you. Some countries, such as Japan, have very strict civil conduct laws: a person with a cold can't go out in public without covering his nose and mouth with a surgical mask!

Even though we can't change other people's personal habits, we can still take certain precautions to build up our resistance to infection. Eating healthful food gives us the vitamins and energy necessary to protect ourselves from the virus. Sleeping well is also helpful, because fatigue prevents us from properly defending our bodies from illness.

You should never hesitate to open the windows of your room, classroom, or anywhere else indoors. This way, you can be sure that the air keeps circulating!

How does my foot fall asleep?

Did you ever feel like your foot was stuffed with pins and needles? Everyone has experienced this funny feeling at least once in life!

Basically, it has to do with the way our bodies' blood circulates. Each time we cross our legs or keep them bent uncomfortably for too long, it squashes our nerves and temporarily slows the circulation of blood in that area.

But your body's heart still beats regularly and the blood flows normally elsewhere in your body, causing a traffic jam! Think of the sand castles we build at the beach: even though we try to protect it using barriers, at one time or another, the waves come crashing through it!

When you uncross your legs or change position, all that blood waiting to circulate engulfs the veins with such force that it irritates our nerve endings and causes an uncomfortable prickly sensation.

Guess it's not pins and needles, after all!

Until normal circulation is restored, there's not much you can do about it: massaging it, dancing around or jumping up and down like a grasshopper won't make it go away any faster!

How does a giant ocean liner float?

Isn't it strange that a 50,000-ton tanker floats in the ocean, but a marble ball sinks in the bathtub?

Archimedes realised how to resolve this enigma while taking a bath. He came out of it crying 'Eureka!' (Greek for 'I've found it!') He discovered that his body weighed less inside the water than out, he seemed to be 'lifted' by the water. This force exerted by the water on the body is now called Archimedes' Principle.

To explain this phenomenon, you have to go back to Greece around 250 BCE. At that time, Hieron, the king of Syracuse, suspected a goldsmith of having swindled him by secretly mixing silver with the gold for his crown. He asked his favourite mathematician, Archimedes, to prove the fraud without damaging the jewel.

When an object is placed in water, it displaces the water, causing the water to rise. The force on an object submerged in water is equal to the weight of the water displaced by the object. If the object is lighter than the displaced water, it floats, because the displaced water obtains the force necessary to keep the object afloat. An object floats as long as its weight is lighter than if it were submerged in water.

A ball filled with glass weighs more than a normal ball filled with water, so it sinks. An ocean liner filled with air weighs less than an ocean liner filled with water, so it floats! A crown made of gold and silver weighs less than a crown made of pure gold, so it takes less time to sink. This is how Archimedes was able to prove to the king that he had been cheated!

'Archimedes, stop doing math in the bathtub!'

How do you think in a foreign language?

Learning to think in another language is not a matter of simply memorising new vocabulary. One must also live among native speakers of the language, and discover their culture first-hand. How do they express their feelings? What makes them laugh?

Words are formed by letters and sounds, and they take on a life of their own. Words are filled with noises, colours, odours, feelings and emotions… a colourful palette that draws on one's experience and imagination, and gives them meaning.

It has been said that people who live in the Artic have at least thirty words for snow, taking into account its colour, shape, the sound it makes under a sled or the hooves of reindeer, and its fragility. As for nomadic Mongols, they draw upon an extensive vocabulary for describing horse-breeding, a subject in which they have great expertise.

You will learn to think in another language the day it becomes so familiar that you stop depending on your maternal language to translate what you want to say.

How can I avoid having to set the table?

Isn't it funny how annoying tasks have a way of repeating themselves? No matter how many excuses you come up with there's no escaping one of the world's worst chores: setting the table!

Why don't you tell yourself how important it is for the family to share their meal together? Or take on the role of the model child: Mom and Dad come home exhausted after a long day at work. Maybe I should give them a hand!

You can even adopt a more communal attitude: the house belongs to all of us, and each person must learn to contribute in every way they can. you're still not convinced, try some math: four forks plus four knives, four glasses and four plates equals? Calculate the total number of tableware items you've set in one year!

The more you distract yourself with fun ideas, the faster you'll set the table! Doesn't it feel good to finish your chores?

Though you may secretly wish that you could eat sandwiches every day of the week, or dine on paper plates, nothing will come of it. So you may as well try to change your attitude about setting the table.

'Whose turn is it to set the table?'

'I'm not here...'

If this last attempt still doesn't do the trick, perhaps you'll succumb to a spirit of adventure: next time you set the table, use chopsticks instead of silverware, old newspapers instead of placemats and coconut shells in place of plates; set the table on the floor and pass around cushions for people to sit on. And if you're feeling more romantic than adventurous, why not dine by candlelight...

How do I know when I'm happy?

Is it possible to be 100 per cent
certain that you are happy?
As sure as 2 + 2 = 4?
No! There's no such thing
as a happiness pill.
It's a personal feeling,
the kind of fulfilment you get
by spending quality time in nature
or bonding with others.

Must one be rich,
powerful, famous,
healthy or in love
to be happy? Not really.
Wealth can disappear
overnight, power can be
ousted and fame
can easily fade!

Wise people think
that we're responsible
for our own happiness,
and that happiness depends
solely on us and not on our
life circumstances. For them,
being happy means renouncing
the pleasures and desires that
would only result in fleeting
happiness. Instead, one must
achieve peace of the mind and
body, which is what true
happiness is all about.

Other
people think that
happiness can only
be achieved when one
makes others happy.
After all, the argument
goes, how can I
be happy when
others suffer?

There are plenty of
theories on 'how to
attain happiness.' But
there is no one formula
that can guarantee it. Don't
spend too much time trying
to find it, or you just might
end up unhappy!

How do boats fit into bottles?

'I said boat, not sailor.'

Are there really tiny little sailors on tiny little boats who sail into tiny little bottles in the sea? Or are there special machines that can form-fit bottles around certain objects?

The answer to both questions is no! To fit a boat into a bottle, you must first choose any old bottle and measure it: its length, width, as well as the diameter of its neck. Next, you must design the boat to fit the bottle's dimensions, just like any object in reduced scale.

The boats found in bottles have some unique characteristics: their masts can be folded in order to fit into the bottle's neck, and by a simple pull of a string, open into place in the bottle itself.

In the beginning of the 19th century, a time of rapid industrial development, glass bottles were produced in vast quantities and became popular items of consumption in markets around the world.

Shortly thereafter, idle sailors at sea and lonely lighthouse keepers came up with the idea of turning these bottles into picture windows! Today, thousands of model boat bottlers around the world keep the traditions of these old navigators alive.

How can carrots make you happy?

Whether or not you like carrots, the moment you bite into one you're reminded of all its great benefits: it gives you rosy cheeks, helps you see in the dark, and makes you feel happy. And the worst part is, it's all true!

In the days of antiquity, Greeks and Romans were well-versed in the therapeutic uses of carrots. However, the reddish-orange root vegetable that we know today was more purplish back then, nearly black, and hard as a rock. They ate them anyway, and extolled (without explaining why) their numerous health benefits.

Even Charlemagne was convinced of the carrot's many benefits; he advised all the monasteries of his empire to add carrots to their soup. Nowadays, carrots, or the carotene contained in them, are a recommended part of one's daily diet.

Carotene is a pigment that the body converts to vitamin A. Vitamin A plays an important role in a number of different ways.

Vitamin A, for example, helps slow the aging of skin cells and naturally protects us from the sun's rays. That's why carrots give us a good complexion. Vitamin A also helps regenerate cells in our liver. People with liver problems are often sad, and suffer from bad moods. By recommending that they eat carrots, not only can they get better, they can also improve their attitude. If you want to be healthy and happy, eat carrots everyday!

Eat your carrots!

19

How can people eat insects?

Parents teach their children what to eat and what not to eat: they make distinctions between healthy food and junk food. Taste is learned and passed down according to culture. Although we may think that insects are gross and scary, some cultures find them tasty, and a major source of protein!

Figuring out what's edible, knowing how to cook it and eating it requires a taste education, which is different for everyone. For children in Burkina Faso, the worms that live in the country's Karite trees early in May are a real treat. They call them the 'caviar of the bush' and there are lots of recipes for how to prepare them – baked or fried!

Crickets, locusts, grasshoppers and caterpillars are also consumed in Asia, Africa or South America.

'Dinner is served!'

bzzz
bzzz
bzzz

But be careful! To practice entomophagy (the eating of insects), you must learn how to differentiate between insects you can eat, and those you can't. For example, you should never eat ladybugs, bed bugs or cockroaches: they're all toxic!

How were castles built without cranes?

Humans have always had more ideas than muscles. Since they first began cultivating the land, humans have made use of all kinds of animals to make up for their physical limitations, inventing machines to do the heavy lifting.

To build castles, workers had to transport large blocks of stone to construction sites using baskets or wheelbarrows pulled by mules, horses or cattle. Once the stones were cut to size, they were placed side by side and fused together using a mixture of lime, sand and grout.

Enough space was left between the stones to insert giant beams on which planks were nailed and pulleys attached. This wooden structure is the precursor to the scaffolding used in construction today. Masons and carpenters were able to build upwards and lift even the heaviest stones using a pulley system.

Once the edifice was constructed, the scaffolding was taken down, and the workers continued along their path in search of more work.

Nowadays, the highest building in the world takes less than a year to build. In the Middle Ages, however, a castle or a cathedral often required several generations of artisans and nearly a century to build.

'Come on, guys, move this stone.'

'um... let's think about it for a few minutes.'

How did people discover that chocolate tasted so good?

According to legend, Quetzalcoatl, the 'feathered serpent' and god of civilisation, taught the Mayas and the Aztecs, two indigenous groups of ancient Mexico, how to cultivate wild cocoa by extracting its beans.

These cocoa beans were crushed and then roasted. The resulting pulp was blended with spices, chilli peppers, cinnamon and aniseed, and then diluted. Because cocoa beans are naturally bitter, the Aztecs added honey to the mixture to sweeten its taste.

The Aztec emperor Montezuma served this beverage, 'xocolatl', while welcoming the Spaniard Hernan Cortés to his land in 1519.

Chocolate made its appearance in 1615, when Anne of Austria, the daughter of the king of Spain, married King Louis XIII of France. Whether it was consumed as medicine or a confectionary, chocolate quickly became popular. From then on, each king appointed his own chocolate maker.

It wasn't until the brutal Spanish conquest of Mexico that the Europeans discovered chocolate. The Spaniards modified the original recipe by replacing the chilli pepper with vanilla beans and adding orange flower. Soon thereafter, they began drinking it hot, and learned to solidify it into tablets for easier transport.

Nowadays, although we no longer thank Quetzalcoatl for his divine offering, everyone knows that chocolate is good for the body and soul!

How can I stop myself from getting angry?

It comes from nowhere. A bit of impatience, some annoyance, the tension builds and, suddenly, it explodes!

Anger often arises when we simply can't achieve something within our reach. Basically, it's the result of frustration. Anger makes our heart beat faster, our hormones rage and our body temperature soar. Just like that! Once it starts, there's little you can do to stop it, short of taking a cold shower! The worst part is that anger not only tires you out, but also leaves you feeling empty and depressed.

Though it may be difficult to control anger, the best tactic is to try to prevent it from spiralling out of control: learn to breathe deeply, for example, and also to talk about it. Even if you might not agree with someone, it doesn't have to lead to a heated argument. You can express your opinion and still listen to another position. This is what healthy debate is all about, and it's the only way to live in society.

The next time your parents tell you to go take your evening bath when you're in the middle of doing something else, instead of throwing a tantrum and yelling 'Wait 5 minutes!' or 'But why!?' and 'You stink!', look them directly in the eyes and use your powers of self-control to calmly explain how you feel. You never know, it just might work! And if it doesn't? Go take your bath!

What is the best way to react to violence?

Is it wise to respond to violence with more violence? To attack others because they have attacked you? Isn't there another solution?

Gandhi, the wise Indian leader, once declared: 'An eye for an eye makes the whole world blind.' Gandhi tolerated neither injustice nor conflict. He believed that the only way to eliminate injustice in the world was to fight it using non-violent means.

Demonstrations, strikes and discussions are non-violent ways to publicly denounce injustice in the world. Martin Luther King in the United States and Nelson Mandela in South Africa fought against racial segregation following Gandhi's example.

All forms of violence, rape and aggression must be denounced. Keeping quiet about it is, essentially, a way of condoning it. Whether you are a victim of or witness to violence, it's possible that you might hesitate to denounce the aggressors for fear of revenge. But isn't it better to let justice handle it?

If you are mistreated at school, for example, why not talk about it with a teacher, a class representative or the principal? Any kind of aggressive act that puts a person in danger is illegal. So when violence of any form occurs, don't hesitate to file a formal complaint to the police, alone or accompanied by an adult.

Should I use my little muscles or not?

When are you considered a genius?

Being a genius means discovering or creating something so original that the world's outlook changes as a result of it.

As beliefs and traditions slowly evolved, a genius was viewed as a sort of hero with magical powers. Nowadays, the status of genius is conferred upon people with extraordinary skills and abilities.

No matter how much talent we're born with, we still have to work hard, because achieving the status of a genius requires a great wealth of knowledge. If you don't apply yourself, study hard and master various techniques, talent may be wasted.

In the past, geniuses weren't often seen in public because it was thought that their godlike minds could radically alter the destiny of those who crossed their paths.

Nevertheless, becoming a genius doesn't happen in a day; it requires effort. For example, even if a child is born with an extremely brilliant mind, he or she'll never become a genius in math if he or she doesn't learn to count! Thomas Edison, the great American inventor, said that genius was '1 per cent inspiration and 99 per cent perspiration.'

History books hail the numerous individuals who have contributed to the evolution of art, science and philosophy. Yet some of those individuals lived miserable lives. Passion and talent combined with lifelong work don't necessarily result in fame. Today's world is full of unknown geniuses. You never know! Perhaps you, too, may be considered a genius some day.

'I'm a genius!'

'Me too'...

'Me too.'

'Same here!'

How can I meet the love of my life?

'One day my prince will come and whisper words of love in my ear…' Storybooks are full of handsome, brave and wealthy princes who gallantly pursue poor princesses. Their strength and determination are proof of true love. How can one resist believing that true love exists?

Fairytales speak to our greatest fears and desires: the fear of never finding love and security and the desire to fall in love and live happily ever after. Fairytales depict a fantasy shared by all people, but they shouldn't be viewed as a guide on how to achieve happiness.

That's why a person shouldn't wait around for their ideal mate to come along in life, like Prince Charming in a fairytale.

There's nothing wrong with dreaming of a great love story. But beware of being disappointed by reality! You can't simply ask someone to embody the role of your childhood hero or heroine; that's not who they are, and that's not what love is.

Don't wait for your true love to come along. That's tantamount to chasing after something that doesn't exist. Be open to any encounter that comes your way. After all, love arrives when you least expect it!

How do babies breathe in their mothers' wombs?

When babies are in their mothers' stomachs, they don't breathe like we do. And although they're floating in fluid, they don't breathe like a fish in water, either.

A foetus' lungs start to develop around the sixth week of pregnancy and become functional around the eighth month. During the last months of pregnancy, a greasy substance is produced to protect the foetus' lungs and prevent them from filling up with liquid. Human lungs are designed to absorb air, and nothing else.

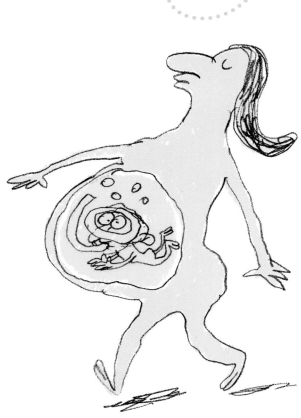

Although a baby's lungs start to function once they're born, their lungs still exhibit respiratory activity in the womb. The umbilical cord attached to the mother contains two arteries and one vein: the vein transports oxygen and nutrients necessary for the foetus' development. The arteries transport carbon dioxide and waste back to the mother. This oxygen/carbon dioxide exchange is what we call breathing.

When the umbilical cord is cut at birth, the newborn must learn to live without his mother's help. In just a few seconds, the lungs open up, the bloodflow quickens and the baby is ready to start functioning on its own. That's what I call a miracle!

Where did fairytales come from?

Fairytales were most likely written to address humans' fear of the unknown. Lightning, thunderstorms, the disappearance of the sun at sunset and its reappearance at dawn seem less frightening when we give them an explanation, even an imaginary one.

Aren't volcanic eruptions less scary when we pretend that they are caused by an underground giant suffering from indigestion? If you live in Japan, where there are frequent earthquakes, isn't it reassuring to imagine that the tremors are caused by a giant jumping from island to island?

Our need to dream and transform everyday occurrences into spectacular events is another explanation for fairytales. In the real world, the strong often defeat the weak and the poor hardly ever get rich overnight.

But anything can happen in the magical world of fairytales. Cinderella, the poor mistreated girl condemned to a life of housework, meets Prince Charming. Little Tom Thumb endures a series of misadventures, including getting kidnapped, before uniting with his family. In fairytales, standard roles are reversed! The weak triumph over the strong and live happily ever after.

Even though various details may differ from culture to culture, fairytale themes are universal.

Let me tell you a story!

How are fireworks made?

'It's my secret recipe!'

Long ago, in China, bamboo was thrown in the fire to scare off Nian, a fierce monster. The bamboo exploded in the fire, creating a loud crackling noise, and causing the evil Nian to flee. This custom may be the origin of modern-day fireworks.

In any case, it was the Chinese who invented the first chemical explosives by combining sulphur, charcoal and saltpetre. This mixture was first used in armies to frighten and kill enemies. Later, it was used to mark celebrations in European courts.

To put on a display of pyrotechnics (the official term for fireworks), a firework engineer makes use of different fuses. The main fuse, which is filled with gunpowder, sets off the smaller fuses, which contain metal granules mixed with explosives.

The latter contain a time-delay fuse that, once ignited, shoots little coloured stars in the sky!

A variety of chemical compounds can be added to the gunpowder to create colours. To obtain blue, copper must be added; to obtain yellow, sodium is mixed in and to attain a golden hue, iron. But in what proportions? Even today, firework engineers fiercely hide their secrets!

What is it like to live in prison?

When a person is convicted of having committed a major crime, there is usually no more appropriate punishment than taking away his or her freedom. Even though it's normal to penalise criminal offenders, spending a lifetime behind bars is no picnic!

Imprisonment means being separated from your family and friends, having no privacy due to overcrowded jails, and having your mail read by others for reasons of security.

In prison, each day is identical: breakfast is served at 7am; dinner is served at 6pm... all under the watchful eyes of the guards.

Hours blend into one another, and it's easy to lose track of time. Days are spent doing repetitive activities: visits, walks in an enclosed space, a bit of physical activity, a visit to the library, reading or writing letters, and, for some, working in a workshop.

'What day is it?'

Even though prisoners can earn a bit of money through paid labour to enrich their daily lives (renting a television, for example, or decorating the walls of their cell), they still live with the strict minimum compared to those in the free world.

How can I prove that video games won't make me stupid?

This can be
an ambitious venture as
very many people
don't know the slightest thing
about video games. And, in fact, seeing
children entirely consumed by the whims
of a revengeful hero will hardly put parents
at ease, especially if they explode
with rage in front of the television.
It's up to you to prove the educational
value of video games to
skeptical adults.

Why not start
by simply showing
them your favourite
game? Explain the rules
and introduce the characters
and the powers they have
at their disposal
basically, describe why
you find this particular
game so intriguing!

However,
beware of going too far.
Your parents aren't fools.
They'll see right through
any attempt to exaggerate
the benefits of video games!
Remember to listen to
their arguments,
and negotiate specific
times during which
video game-playing
will be allowed.

Excess of
any kind is bad.
In this case, staring at
a screen for hours on
end can have a hypnotic
effect: you may enter a state
in which you become
completely oblivious to
your surroundings and
find it hard to wake up
to reality.

Why not ask one of
your parents to play a game
with you? You never know…
With a bit of patience and indulgence,
you may have found yourself
a decent opponent!

How are babies made?

Adults didn't always like having to answer this question. They thought it wasn't appropriate for children, since it deals with sexual relations between a man and a woman.

As a result, all kinds of crazy stories have been told about where babies come from. Either a stork brings it home, or it was found in a cabbage patch, or rosebushes. But what is more natural than the birth of a child?

From a purely biological standpoint, two specific cells must come together to make a baby: the male cell, called spermatozoa, which is produced in the father's genitalia, and the female cell, the ovum, or egg, which is in the mother.

A natural pathway was designed in the woman's body for the father's sperm to reach the mother's ovum. The fusion of the two cells forms a tiny egg – an embryo –, which develops over the course of nine months and is delivered as a baby.

'I get no respect.'

'Oh no, not the stork again!'

But the birth of a child involves a lot more than just biology. 'Making' a baby has a lot to do with chance, because one sperm among millions must penetrate the ovum to create an embryo. And choosing to make a baby in the first place depends on a man and a woman making a joint decision to create a new life.

Perhaps we should rephrase the question and ask 'How is life created?' After all, that's what it is all about!

34

How do we know what the future will hold?

For millennia, humans have wondered what life had in store for them: luck or misfortune? They wanted to know what lay before them in order to influence – or succumb – to their destiny. What waited around the corner? Sickness? Love? Death?

Throughout the world, people have questioned the stars, precious stones, and even seashells to uncover clues about their future. In China, over 4,000 years ago, soothsayers used the shape and patterns on a turtle's shell to predict their emperor's future. All in all, these methods have proven useless in attempting to shed light on man's destiny.

'I see, I see, I see...

that it's time to get my eyes checked!'

Is it easier to predict the future of a planet? For example, figuring out how it will look several hundred years from now? A number of scientists are trying to determine the future of the earth based on present-day observations. They take into account climate change, global warming, desert formation, deforestation, earthquakes, etc...

But even in these cases, their predictions are based on working hypotheses regarding the evolution of our planet. No one can say with any degree of certainty what the earth will be like tomorrow, even if it depends a great deal on how we treat it today! No matter what, it's impossible to know what the future holds!

How do plants grow in the desert?

The plants that we see in the desert are true heroes! To grow, they have to fight against dryness, withstand extremely high daytime temperatures and cold nighttime temperatures, and make do with soil rich in salt and low in fertiliser.

Three main types of plants have adapted to these conditions, each in its own way: annuals, phraetophytes and xerophytes. Annuals are very patient: their seeds can survive for three years without water and still bloom. It's easy to see why they're called 'dormant'! Annuals spring to life for a period of only a few weeks, and only during one season.

Phraetophytes grow a network of long underground roots from which new ones sprout. Because they are deeply entrenched in the ground, they resist extreme heat as well as sandstorms. They flower every other year.

Xerophytes are known for their extreme resistance to drought. These plants absorb and store the tiniest drop of water. A cactus is perhaps the most well-known member of this group. After a rain shower in the desert, a big cactus can absorb many litres of water, and stock a reserve for the dry months that lay ahead. Now that's heroic!

'What am I doing here...?'

How do painters see the world?

Sometimes, when we look at portraits painted by Picasso, Chagall, or Duchamp, or landscapes painted by Matisse or Van Gogh, we may wonder if these painters had problems with their vision! Have you ever seen a triangle-shaped nose, a head bigger than the body it's attached to, or purple trees?

But painters don't wear special glasses! Art isn't a question of sight but of observation and interpretation. Even if two painters went to the same art school, had the same teachers, spent the same number of hours working on their technique, and used the same props or models, their paintings still wouldn't look alike.

'Hello Mr. Picasso. How do you do?'

Try this experiment with your brothers and sisters: take a piece of paper and crayons and draw a picture of your family. Now compare your results. You'll notice that the difference between your drawing and those of your brothers and sisters is the result of the unique way in which you see your family. Maybe you've sketched yourself as being taller than your older brother; your younger sister may not even have bothered to include you!

Each human being is unique, and the same goes for the way he or she sees the world. One person's sense of reality is very different from another's, which is why we can't reproduce it.

The same thing goes for painters: rather than try to capture reality on a canvas, they paint their ideas and perceptions the world.

What does it mean to be successful in life?

Your teachers and parents may have given you the impression that getting good grades is the key to a successful life. By that logic, the best student in class would be the most successful later on in life.

However, even if knowledge and competence can help you land a job and achieve a certain level of success, they aren't the sole prerequisites of being successful!

Fortunately, a successful life is not measured by how many diplomas you receive, nor by the profession you choose, and least of all by the amount of money you have in your bank account...Success can't be planned too far in advance. There isn't a single pathway leading toward fame and fortune.

So what does it mean to have a successful life? It's a personal feeling more than anything else: living a life that includes everything you always hoped for. A successful life incorporates everything: our relationships with other people and our experiences, our knowledge and convictions, as well as the mistakes, doubts and failures that make us human.

It takes time to succeed in life. Gandhi, the spiritual and political leader of India, fought against racism, religious discrimination and violence until his death. For him, success in life meant fighting until the end.

How can some children live with only one parent?

'One parent...

is largely sufficient!'

Our birth required the joint participation of a man and a woman, our biological parents. Our continued growth and development requires, more than anything else, a stable and loving environment, be it in the presence of one parent, or both, or our adoptive parents.

Each case is unique. That's why it's so hard to come up with a general answer. When you live with only one parent, it may sometimes feel that your family has overcome a turbulent past. But it doesn't mean that you've lived off on your own, completely cut off from the outside world.

Children are free to reach outside their circle of family and friends and find whatever they lack in the way of affection, knowledge and comfort.

The difficulty of being the child of a single parent is having to take on the role of a 'little man' or a 'little woman.' For example, a single mother may call her son 'my little man' or a father might choose to discuss his grown-up problems with his daughter.

But a child should only have one role in the life of his or her parents, namely, that of a child – one that needs security, love, recreation, education and a social life. Children should never have to fill a hole in the lives of their parents. Sometimes as hard as it is for children to stand up for their rights, it's absolutely necessary for a healthy childhood.

Where do ideas come from?

A lot has been said
about the origin of ideas.
Are we born with a neat little
suitcase of ideas, which we can search
through to figure out how best
to structure our comprehension
of the world?

It's
hard
to say exactly how
ideas form in
our brains, or how we
use them to express
ourselves coherently.

Do ideas
come from
what we see,
hear, taste, feel and
touch, combined
in new ways?

Actually,
our senses help us to be
imaginative, inventive, creative,
and generate new ideas.
But we use our reasoning
to arrange our perceptions
of the world.

Being
curious,
observing
the world around us
(for example, nature),
reading, debating,
travelling, meeting
new people and
discovering works
of arts – this is what
inspires new ideas.

Therefore,
the more you ask questions
and challenge yourself to find
answers to them on your own,
the more ideas you'll have. After all,
there are no bad ideas, just a lack of will
to execute them!

How do whales sing?

Like other animal languages, the language whales use to communicate with one another is made up of codes and signals: wags of the tail or fins, acrobatic movements under the water, noisy dives, as well as calls and whistles.

Even though both males and females are capable of producing sounds to communicate, only the male whales sing – during the mating season (in order to seduce the females) and during the winter migration.

Some whales can sing for over 15 minutes without taking a breath. Oh, the things we do for love! Females can hear these declarations of love from far away, thanks to sound waves emitted by these calls, which travel through the water.

Bravo!

Each year, at the end of the mating season, male whales may learn a new song from the other whales, and add it to their song repertory. Every five years or so, their melodies change completely.

Singing whales don't tire easily: their concerts can last for hours, even days, on end. This way they can seduce even the most stubborn females!

can God hear us?

Does God have big ears, like radars, that can hear the messages we send Him? No matter which religion you belong to, picturing God has always been a challenge.

Many humans believe in a God created in their own image, with a face, body and feelings. This gives them a mental image during prayer.

But if we humans can talk to God, how can God hear us? For those who believe in God, the word 'hear', which also means 'listen' and 'understand,' shows that God is not indifferent to them. God is ever-present, even though He's invisible.

Believers feel that God is close to them and brings meaning to their lives. It is this particular reciprocity between man and God that is so special and so vital.

How are tunnels built underwater?

With a pick and a shovel! Ok, but that might take a while! Digging a tunnel underwater follows the same principle as drilling a tunnel through a mountain, except you have to dig very deep to get under the marine floor.

Digging underneath the earth's surface requires a kind of giant mechanical mole: a tunnel-boring machine. This is a giant cylinder set up on tracks whose rotating head is so powerful it can pound through even the toughest rock. The conveyor belts to either side of the cylinder function as arms which clear away loosened material from the excavated earth. The rock-face is covered in either concrete or metal to stabilise the tunnel walls and avoid landslides.

A tunnel-boring machine can dig more than 61 metres per day. That's a lot! But a mole, which weighs a mere five ounces, can dig up to 19 metres a day! Given its small stature, that's quite a feat!

One of the longest underground tunnels in the world today is the Euro tunnel, which links France and Great Britain through the English Channel. It measures just over 48 kilometres in length and can be crossed by train in just 20 minutes at speeds of up to 160 kilometres an hour.

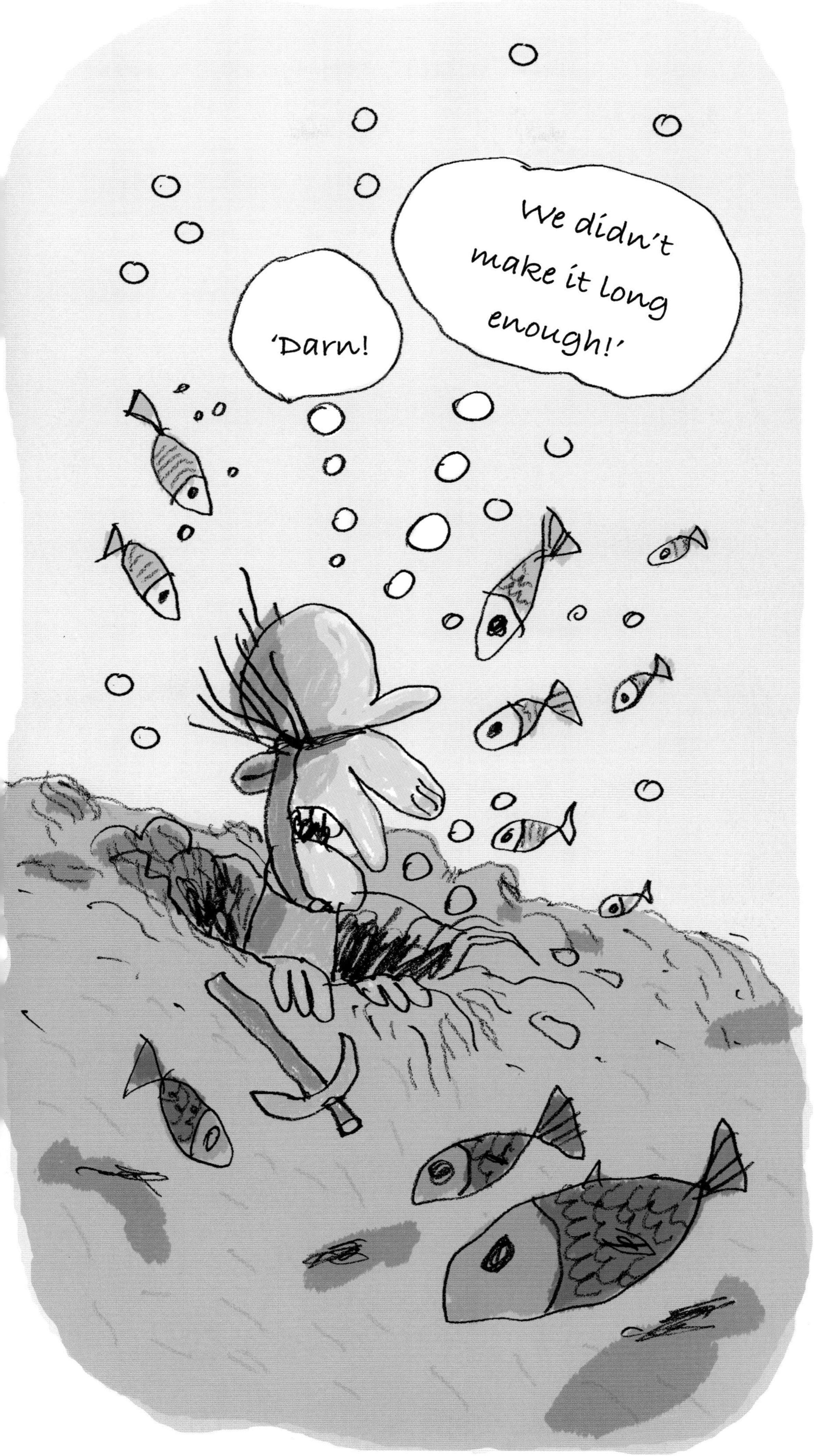
'Darn!
We didn't make it long enough!'

How were colours made before paint tubes existed?

According to some estimates, humans began to draw around 40,000 years ago, even though they started to write only 3,000 years ago! Drawing and painting play an integral role in the human need to express oneself.

In the Stone Age, humans already knew how clay, ashes from bones and vegetal pigments could be mixed with water or grease to obtain paints suitable for drawing on rock faces or cave walls. We continue to be awed by the beauty of those early paintings still today, in every part of the world.

'Where would I be without my paint set...?'

Throughout history, various civilisations actively sought out colours vibrant enough to pay homage to the beauty of their god or gods. They dug through the soil to obtain browns, reds and yellows; minerals gave them greens and blues; chalk and clay produced whites; even seashells yielded colours such as crimson.

Much like chefs, painters have their own recipes for enhancing their colours and diversifying their palettes. The precious powders obtained from the earth's soil can be used as they are, or heated and mixed with water, egg whites, or oils.

Even though some painters prefer to use these more artisan techniques to derive their paints, the development of more industrial techniques have led to the production of paints in every shade of the rainbow. But don't let that stop you from experimenting, so you can create your own unique colours!

How do people go crazy?

Word like 'crazy' and 'insane' are used daily to describe everything that falls outside the realm of sensibility or normal behaviour. But experts see insanity as something far more serious: it starts when a person finds it increasingly difficult to live in society because he or she feels, either consciously or unconsciously, that he or she no longer belongs.

The biological factor: our brain is an extremely complex organ charged with the task of processing all kinds of information, thanks to an elaborate network of connected cells. Sometimes, however, certain cells can't connect, or become disconnected, resulting in abnormal or dangerous behaviour towards oneself or others.

Insanity isn't a sickness that we can catch, like a cold. Rather, it's a troubling mental condition caused by a number of different factors.

'I'm crazy about you, doctor!'

A person may also become more withdrawn, due to negative influences stemming from his or her social or familial environment. In this case, his or her illness is caused by psychological factors.

Many such illnesses, such as depression, schizophrenia, or narcolepsy have been diagnosed in varying degrees of severity. Some can be treated successfully, others not. But medication and other forms of treatment have been used by doctors and therapists to ease a patient's suffering.

Craziness and insanity aren't labels under which all kinds of abnormal behaviour should be categorised. Remember, there's a big difference between eccentricity and illness!

How can I satisfy my curiosity?

You might think of curiosity as a flaw, especially if you find yourself tearing through someone else's belongings or peering through a keyhole. But without curiosity, we might not even be here!

Potatoes were discovered by digging up the ground; the magnifying glass was invented in order to see the tiniest known particles; and rockets were designed to enable us to bring back parts of the moon. Since the beginning of time, human have always looked beyond what's in front of themselves, whether it be to discover new lands or to better understand their environment.

Humans created the notions of gods and spirits to explain death, illness and meteorological phenomena, by resorting to their fertile imagination. But some people weren't satisfied and came up with their own, theoretical, explanations.

Discovery often arises as a result of dissatisfaction. In questioning established beliefs, we create an opportunity whereby new explanations are possible.

To prove that there is reason to doubt something, one must first come up with an alternative theory and put it through a number of tests until it becomes accepted as the new rule, susceptible to its own scrutiny in the future. In the past, the earth was thought to be flat…

Great discoveries always shocked the established order of the day and history is full of explorers and inventers who were scorned during their lifetime. And yet, we are where we are today thanks to them and their many trials and errors.

How is striped toothpaste made?

Whether they're red, green or blue, toothpaste stripes have no apparent function other than making the toothpaste look prettier and thus persuading consumers to buy one brand over another. But regardless of how they look, how did the stripes get in the tube in the first place?

There's no magic in toothpaste stripes, only one thing to keep in mind: the nozzle of a toothpaste tube is fitted with a special device, several millimetres in length and pierced with a ring of small holes. Unlike a normal tube filled end to end with white paste, striped toothpaste contains two other compartments on each side filled with coloured paste.

When the tube is squeezed, the white paste pushes on the compartments of coloured paste, which in turn pushes through the holes in the tube's nozzle. Thin ribbons of colour attach themselves to the white paste, producing a striped pattern.

To better understand the mechanics of how it works cut a toothpaste tube in half, lengthwise, and see for yourself!

How pretty!

How was the earth discovered to be round?

'I know it seems strange ...but you'll have to get used to it!'

A disk floating on the sea, an egg, a pear, a pine cone, or a rounded cylinder: almost all of these descriptions have been used at one time or another to describe the shape of the earth before it was entirely explored.

In the days of Greek antiquity, wise men claimed that the earth was round, but no one believed them. However, they noticed that when travelling from north to south, the star constellations usually present in the sky would disappear, and others would appear in their place.

Much later, a voyage sailed off to circumnavigate the globe. The expedition of Ferdinand Magellan, which left Spain on September 20, 1519, cleared up any remaining doubts: his ships travelled from west to east and arrived at the same spot three years later, without ever turning around.

Magellan and his crew thus made the first tour of the world, proving once and for all that the earth was round. Before their trip, unanimity had never been reached regarding the earth's shape. Because man saw himself as being the centre of the universe, the earth was thought to be a flat plate surrounded by ocean! Then again, without any form of verification, everything seems possible!

How can we be sure we've found true love?

Your heart beats faster when you hear his or her voice. You blush when he or she looks at you. You stutter and stumble over your words even though you had a whole speech prepared…It's pretty clear from these scenarios that love has taken hold of you. But how can you be sure that it's true love, love with a capital L, the kind that lasts a lifetime?

Lust and love are two very different emotions. Lust is linked to immediate desires and pleasure. You may hardly know a person, and yet they have cast a spell over you, inspiring a kind of giddy excitement. You find yourself dreaming of them, or imagining them in different scenarios; in fact, you project your own desires on them, without taking into account their own.

Being in love is a different story. Love takes time to grow and requires that two people truly know each other. The dreaminess is still there, but it's a dream shared by two people, who walk along the same path, hand in hand. You love and are loved in return, and find it difficult to imagine life without the other.

But whether you are in lust or love, there's no guarantee that the other person feels the same way. And so? Well, what's nice about love is that, in the end, you can never be sure about anything. That's why it's so important to be careful, don't jump into anything too fast, and always be in touch with your inner feelings.

'Uh, I hope it's not contagious.'

ugga, ugga, ugga

How were museums invented?

Humans have long had a tendency to collect souvenirs. Children pile their treasures in boxes hidden under their beds. Adults accumulate possessions. Countries build museums.

Prehistoric caves were discovered to contain sculpted bones, pebbles and seashells. Egyptians accumulated all kinds of precious objects as a way of embellishing their afterlife.

From the time of Antiquity through the Middle Ages, princes and religious figures from different civilisations assembled a large number of works of art in their temples and churches for the benefit of the public.

Starting in the 16th century, aristocratic Italian families set an example for all the other European courts by assembling collections of rare objects, thereby initiating the artistic movements of their time. But these were not yet museums, only private collections.

Little by little, these rare objects and works of art began to be classified by genre and date, and were dedicated to the halls of the great palaces, called 'galleries'. Artists and students, chosen at random, were invited to come and admire them. In France, during the Revolution, these buildings and collections were nationalised, and displayed to the general public. Hence, the first museums were born.

How was it decided that a week would consist of seven days?

To better organise life in society, humans had to find a way to structure their time according to their work schedule or seasonal changes. Thanks to their keen sense of observation, the calendar was invented.

'What day is it today?'

The moon orbits the earth about once every 28 days, and goes through various phases: new moon, first quarter, full moon and third quarter. When you divide these 28 days by these four phases, you get a period of seven days: one week.

The Chaldeans of Babylonia were the first to perform this division, in around 500 before our current era, and adapt it to their daily lives.

After them, the Hebrews gave it religious significance by drawing on the Bible, which stipulates that God created the world in six days, and rested on the seventh. This seventh day corresponds to the Sabbath in Jewish tradition.

But it was in Rome, under the emperor Augustus, that the week as we know it today was definitively adopted. Each day (or diem in Latin) was correlated to a different planet and named after it: Moon (Monday), Mars (Tuesday), Mercury (Wednesday) Jupiter (Thursday) Venus (Friday) Saturn (Saturday) and the Sun (Sunday).

English has retained the original planet names for only three of its days: Monday, Saturday and Sunday.

54

Is justice fair?

Justice refers to the principle of equality between individuals. As an institution, justice mediates conflicts between individuals and permits each individual to exercise his or her rights. But can victims influence justice, by what is written in the media or by the opinions of others? Is there a type of justice that applies solely to the rich, and another to the poor? In other words, is justice truly just?

Justice is an institution administered by the state, but judges don't depend on it for their ruling. They judge by way of their soul and their conscience by looking at all the facts presented and the responsibility and actions of those accused. They never give in to pressure. And the government cannot influence their decisions.

'It's not fair!'

If judges make mistakes, then 'judicial errors' can be recognised, but this is very rare. One should have faith in the system of justice which exists to protect the fundamental rights of each person: the right to freedom, life, and security; the right to leave one's country and return to it; the right to practice one's religion; the right to speak one's mind, and the right to information.

In dictatorships, in which the government controls everything, justice is no longer independent but rather directed by the arbitrary authority of its rulers. Rather than guaranteeing rights, this system of justice denies fundamental rights to its citizens.

How can I explain to my family that my room is private?

'Do not enter!' The sign is written clearly on the door!!! But there's nothing you can do to enforce it. It's hard to create your own little niche, where shoes, apple cores, empty soda cans, photos, books, disks and secret drawers all co-exist happily, in a state of complete disorder.

Although people in the West seek privacy, that may not always hold true for people in other societies, in which family members of all ages can live together in the same room. Private space is relative depending on culture. But it's fair to say that at one time or another, each person seeks a little peace and quiet.

For millennia, humans have created boundaries between their world and the exterior world, between inside and out, public and private. There are rules in all societies governing when your entry is permitted in certain places, and when it's not. The need to call a room one's own – a small enclosed private space – has stood the test of time.

You want your family to respect the privacy of your room because you consider it your little corner of freedom – an escape from communal living. And why not! Nobody ought to go into your closet, drawers or other hidden places when you're not there.

It all comes down to trust between parents and children, brothers and sisters. But don't forget about reciprocity: other people's bedrooms are also private!

How do birds see us from high up in the sky?

They see us as big, dangerous, unappetising, two-footed beasts! No, seriously, from up high, birds see us just as clearly as though they were looking at us through binoculars.

Birds don't have a handicap when it comes to their vision, even when they're flying high up in the sky. They have more visual cells per square millimetre than humans do, so their vision is eight times better. Some species have a perfect 360-degree field of vision!

Like us, birds can distinguish colours, but they appear far more vivid to them because they can see ultraviolet, whereas we can't.

Birds have a better sense of direction than we do and faster instincts in times of danger (obstacles or predators). Do these master seers have any faults? Yes! Apparently, some birds are scared of the colour blue! Maybe that will make us feel better about our poor vision...

'Excuse me sir! Your fly is open!'

How can we be certain that we're not living in a dream?

Is our life nothing but a dream – an illusion? What if we were like Alice in Wonderland or Pinocchio, imaginary characters straight out of a fairytale? We might think we were real, but we would actually be living in a world of fiction.

When we're asleep, we can't always tell the difference between dreams and reality. The people we see, the adventures we embark on and the emotions we feel when we're dreaming may seem very real.

A long time ago, an old Chinese sage by the name of Chuang Tzu said: 'I dreamed that I was a butterfly, and when I woke up I wondered whether I was a man who dreamed he was a butterfly, or a butterfly dreaming he was a man.' Is it that easy to confuse dreams and reality?

As we grow and our brains continue to develop, we learn to distinguish dreams from reality. Once we become adults, we see things a lot more clearly, and there's no more room for confusion.

Everyone creates his or her own little world in dreams, kind of like a film set, which differs from one person to another. In the real world, on the other hand, everyone perceives the same things — the same landscape, the same city… and this general perception never changes. Whatever dreams may come to me at night, I know that once I open my eyes, everything will be exactly as it was when I first closed them…

How do fish sleep?

How do
fish sleep when they
get tired of swimming?
Under a bedspread
or down comforter?
On a bed of algae?
Inside a shell?

Do fish actually sleep or
are they merely pretending to?
They never seem to tire of staring at
us with their big eyes. And for good
reason! Fish don't have eyelids;
a transparent membrane covers
their eyes, like a pair of tiny
scuba-diving goggles!

So, if you happen
to see a fish perfectly still,
almost immobile, lulled by
the gentleness of the
river's current, chances are
it's taking a short rest.
Whatever you do, try not
to disturb him!

zzz zzz zzz zzz zzz zzz zzz zzz

How can I say what I feel?

There are times when you don't dare interrupt a discussion in progress for fear of others' judgments and opinions. You might be afraid to say something stupid or stumble over your words, so you choose to say nothing, thereby giving the illusion of indifference.

'John John, you're an [card] !'

But why keep quiet when you don't agree with something? Though you may run the risk of being judged, talked back to, or even insulted, it is still important to speak your mind and stick up for what you believe in. This is what healthy debate is all about.

A good way to overcome your fear of speaking is to clarify your ideas in your mind first, before you begin to speak. Remembering to take deep breaths is also important when you want to express your opinions calmly, without aggression, and defend them using two or three simple arguments.

But be careful! Words can be a formidable weapon, so you'll want to think before you speak and measure the consequences of doing so, so as not to offend or humiliate anyone. Saying exactly what you feel is not an invitation to harm others, but to respect them.

Avoid long-winded monologues, loud interruptions or slamming doors. After all, you aren't acting in a play, and these antics won't make you popular with your listeners. You must learn to accept other opinions and criticism, but not at the cost of abandoning your own position.

How was music invented?

To explain how music came about, a number of legends purport that the gods were the musicians of their time: in Greece, Apollo played the lyre; in India, Sri Krishna preferred the flute…These divine beings were generous with their art, but for good reason: they taught men how to play instruments, so they, in turn, could play for them.

Others believe that music, as indicated by its name, was a gift from the Muses. They say that these Greek goddesses turned music, poetry and dance into an art form, so we could sing their praises and give them cult status. Sacred music linked the world of the gods with that of the mortals.

Legends aside, prehistoric humans understood early on that tapping on a shell, pebble, bamboo branch or taut animal fur produced very different sounds. The pleasure they derived from this experiment, coupled with the effect of the produced sounds, made it tempting to repeat and continually harmonise them.

Much time passed before instruments capable of reproducing the sounds of the wind, water and birdcalls were created. The Egyptian harp, for example, is only about 5,000 years old.

How can I be accepted in a group?

Being part of a group brings about feelings of security and recognition, but it might foster dependency, uniformity and a loss of freedom. In fact, groups have the unfortunate tendency of being exclusive and therefore intolerant of difference, change, and the unknown.

Wanting at all costs to be integrated in a certain group is not a trivial matter: before you jump in, it's best to inquire about the mentality of the group and understand your motivation for wanting to join it.

Joining a group requires that you prove yourself, and your intentions, to the members. This may not be such a simple task. Your fear of being judged, and the ensuing lack of self-confidence under the circumstances, may mask your true personality and lend a bad impression.

The most agreeable groups are those that are often the most open-minded, for example teams that revolve around sports, games or art. A strong team is one that sets out to achieve a common goal, with each of its members contributing in a significant way.

'So??

Do I make the cut?'

So try your best to overcome your shyness and prove your value and self-worth to others. Despite your best intentions, the group may still deny you access either because there's no space left, or because they simply fear what they don't know. But don't let that get you down! After all, there's nothing preventing you from going out and starting your own group!

How can people live without love?

Hunger cries, childish fears, adolescent rebellion and adult anguish – all these forms of human distress have one thing in common: a feeling of abandonment, caused by a lack of love.

Some parents are incapable or unsure of how to properly love their child, so much so that the child may go through life feeling unloved. This kind of treatment can cause serious injury to the child, and prevent him or her from growing up securely.

But what's the point of growing up when nobody respects or cares for you? An unloved child may never develop confidence in him or herself, and could spend the rest of his or her life yearning for love.

Sometimes, however, people can develop the patience, affection and tenderness to make up for their difficult upbringing. They may start to believe in others, because others took the time to believe in them.

But whether you're a child or an adult, it's impossible to live without love. Love gives us an identity, makes us feel respected and enriches our lives.

How were national flags invented?

Regardless of their shape or colour, flags once served as the civil or military emblems of a tribe, lord, family or an entire city. They functioned as a kind of 'business card', showing visitors exactly who ruled there.

In the past, flags were used to announce a state of quarantine (for example, when a city was in the throes of an epidemic). In the nautical world, coloured flags hoisted on masts allowed boats to communicate with one another over long distances. Warning flags went up immediately if pirate ships were known to be in the vicinity!

When countries were founded, standards flags were transformed into national flags. Every nation in the world is identified by its own unique flag. The colours and the references incorporated on them are symbols dating from a country's history.

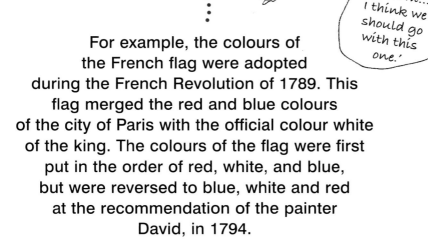

'Hmmm... I think we should go with this one.'

For example, the colours of the French flag were adopted during the French Revolution of 1789. This flag merged the red and blue colours of the city of Paris with the official colour white of the king. The colours of the flag were first put in the order of red, white, and blue, but were reversed to blue, white and red at the recommendation of the painter David, in 1794.

How do children train to become soldiers?

War has killed nearly two million children since 1990, destroyed schools and wiped out entire villages. Six million children have been injured and at least a million orphaned.

Today, 300,000 child soldiers fight in armed conflicts in more than thirty conflicts around the world. These statistics – made public by UNICEF in December 2004 – are staggering.

The majority of child soldiers are drugged to numb them to fear and violence. Whether they live in Burma, Africa, the Philippines, Latin America or Sri Lanka, child soldiers are usually recruited by rebel groups fighting against the government.

These child soldiers fight on wars' frontlines, machine-guns in hand. Sometimes they're as young as eight years old and forced to commit atrocities.

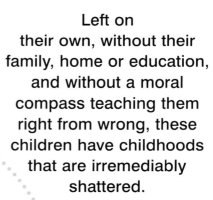

Left on their own, without their family, home or education, and without a moral compass teaching them right from wrong, these children have childhoods that are irremediably shattered.

A number of child protection organisations have called upon the United Nations to punish countries that enlist soldiers under the age of eighteen for crimes against humanity.

How do blind people read?

Blind people read with their hands. In 1821, Louis Braille learned about a system called 'night writing' used by the army in the beginning of the 19th century; this system enabled soldiers to read and share secret messages in the dark, without being seen by the enemy. Braille realised that this system could be adapted for use by the blind. After having lost his sight at the age of 3, Braille studied at the school for the blind in Paris, where he became a teacher.

'I have eyes on my fingertips.'

The system of Braille is made up of 64 combinations of raised dots made by a special stylus or typewriter. These combinations cover every letter of the alphabet, accented vowels, punctuation signs, numbers, mathematical signs and even musical notes.

Reading is achieved by touching the embossed type with one's fingertips, from left to right, just like normal reading. Braille is a complete reading and writing system using 6 dots in different positions in a rectangular cell (a maximum of 2 dots from top to bottom and 3 across).

Braille has been adapted to almost every language, including Chinese. But many texts have yet to be transcribed into Braille. Greater progress is needed, so that the blind have more access to great works of literature.

For example, the letter A is symbolised by a dot in the upper left-hand corner of the rectangular cell; to obtain the letter B, a second dot is added underneath the one written for A.

How do roosters know when to crow?

A rooster crows as soon as it wakes up to impress the chickens in the poultry yard. But little does he know that he performs the function of an alarm clock for the people around him!

Before the invention of the light bulb, farms operated according to the rhythm of the days. People, like animals, organised their days around sunlight: they woke up and went to bed at the same time as the sun.

As soon as his eyes open, the rooster takes his place on the roof of the chicken coop and crows to whoever will listen that he is best and most beautiful of them all. And woe to those who attempt to step into his territory! For the most part, the rooster awakens at dawn. Therefore, the rooster's crow announces to all that it's time to wake up.

Unfortunately, sometimes a loud noise or a bout of insomnia might awaken the rooster prematurely, prompting him to crow in the middle of the night! Farmers, exhausted by these untimely wake-ups, have learned to rely on their alarm clocks for their wake-up call, rather than trust these self-appointed 'rulers' of the chicken coop.

How do I ask for forgiveness?

Crash!
Your football has just
shattered the neighbour's
window! Yikes! After a stupid
stunt like that, you may
feel like running away,
becoming invisible,
or worse, blaming it
on another person.
'I didn't do it!
He did it…'

Nobody's perfect!
Clumsiness is excusable, and
it's always best to try to repair the
damage. On the other hand, when
you deliberately blame another person
for your own mistake, it's no longer
a stupid stunt; it's an injustice.
How can you ask for forgiveness
from someone you've wrongfully
accused? That can be awkward!
It's not easy to admit making a
mistake; you'll probably hear lots
of bad excuses before a person
can admit that he has hurt
someone else.

Asking
for forgiveness
requires courage and
sincerity. It's always best
to use simple words and
affectionate gestures to renew
ties with those you've hurt,
rather than a long, drawn-out
apology. What's essential is
that you feel responsible
for your acts and prove
your good faith in order to
regain their trust.

But making
amends to those you've
betrayed is the only way to
regain their trust. The words
and actions you use to excuse
yourself should be accompanied
by a promise that you won't
repeat the same
mistake!

How can we know what happens after we die?

For millennia, men have feared the unknown. As a result, they try to explain what they don't understand, such as the passage between life and death.

They've wondered about the survival of the soul: does the soul live on after the body decomposes? Do the dead embark on a whole new life? Can they communicate with us? Do they have any influence over the world of the living?

Many people thought that the dead went to either heaven or hell. They thought of life as continuing into the afterworld, and that the dead could make contact with the living.

In Africa, according to traditional beliefs, the dead live side by side with the living. They see us, protect us and can seek revenge upon us if we forget them. As for the Hindus, they believe in reincarnation, the notion that the dead come back to life as another human, animal or vegetal form, until they attain perfection.

'Is that all there is?'

All faiths – Buddhism, Judaism, Christianity, Islam and Hinduism – believe that life doesn't end at death. Death is viewed as a necessary pathway to a new life, one that is better and closer to God. But, alas, these are only hopes, not certainties.

How can we avoid going to school?

School is mandatory until the age of at least sixteen, so you have no choice but to attend. Even if you complain of a stomachache the day of a big exam, there's no avoiding the fact that at one time or another, you have to go back to class!

The first known systems of education date from about 4,000 before our current era. Obviously, humans' need to educate themselves didn't begin yesterday! In England, the Elementary Education Act in 1880 made schooling compulsory, giving each person the right to an education.

Free, secular, public schools can't impose any specific mode of thinking on its student body. These schools promote free thinking, by teaching the basics of communication, thought and reflection.

Sprinting to school in the mornings out of excitement to learn new things isn't exactly normal, but neither is hating it to the point where you refuse to step foot in the classroom. Disliking school is the result of more profound reasons: the fear of failure, or ranking last in the class; the fear of getting picked on or insulted if you don't understand a certain exercise; or even fear of verbal attack.

Whatever the reason, a solution must be found to remedy the situation. Cutting class isn't the answer! If your fear of school is so strong that you wish to avoid it altogether, talk about it with your parents or a trustworthy teacher. They're there to lend a helping hand.

How do glow-worms light up?

Humans have long depended on artificial light to find their way in the dark. At first they used fire and eventually, electricity. But when it comes to lighting, there is one bug with far more expertise than us: glow-worms.

The glow-worm belongs to the firefly family, which possesses special light organs located on the underside of the abdomen.

At certain times of the night, particularly during the mating period in the summertime, the glow-worm emits an enzyme called 'luciferase' which, when combined with oxygen, generates light. The female glow-worm, which cannot fly, signals her presence to the male by flickering her light. This way, the couple can find each other in the dark.

'Ah, how you make me glow!'

In South Asia, some species of fireflies meet in trees by the thousands and flash on and off, all night long…

How can I make friends?

A new school, new neighbourhood, new state…one day you may find yourself in a completely new world where nobody knows you and you may begin to feel very alone…Though your parents may tell you that it's only temporary, the prospect of not having any friends can be terrifying.

Then again, how many times a day do you greet a stranger with a simple 'Hello?' More often than you realise. This greeting – this first casual 'Hello' – opens the door to getting to know someone better.

But a simple 'How do you do?' is not enough. To make a friend, you have to develop certain ties with that person. This requires time and effort. Having a friend demands responsibility. So is there some kind of magic recipe for making friends?

Greeting someone has always been, in every culture, a sign of peace. Even a long time ago, a courteous greeting proved that one came as a friend, not an enemy.

The short answer is: no. Friendship is based on the mutual sharing of belongings, complicity and forgiveness, because there is no such thing as a perfect friend.

Hello! Hello! Hello! Hello! Hello! Hello! Hello! Hello!

The great writer Montaigne, when asked how he chose his friends, replied: 'Because I'm me and he's he…' That's a pretty good way of summarising the mystery of friendship, don't you think?

74

How does a veterinarian know where an animal hurts?

Aside from fables and fairytales, lions and sheep don't talk, and they certainly don't complain of a sore throat! Does this mean that veterinarians are fluent in the language that animals use to communicate?

Not really. But their many years of schooling helped them develop expertise in how animals function. And they've also learned a thing or two about the various illnesses that can afflict animals.

When the problem is obvious – such as when an animal gets a pebble stuck in its paw, making it limp – the diagnosis is easy to make. But sometimes the cause of an animal's ailment is more complex, and a more thorough examination is required.

In this case, the veterinarian might ask the owner questions about the animal's habits, and whether the animal's behaviour has changed recently. Has it lost its appetite? Does it seem agitated? Aggressive? Or, on the contrary, more withdrawn?

The answers to these questions give the veterinarian clues as to what the animal's symptoms might be. Veterinarians also rely on precious instruments and imaging – such as X-rays and ultrasounds – which help them figure out what's ailing an animal.

How can I avoid pastries?

Having a sweet tooth isn't a problem, unless it starts to affect your weight and health. One of the most difficult things is learning how to resist excess: excess cake, candy, TV and video games. Otherwise, you'll end up with indigestion! Just as the wise ancient Greeks used to say: the right amount is that which everyone agrees on. No more, no less.

To avoid pastries, all you have to do is steer clear of pastry shops along your path, either by turning around or quickly crossing the street when you see one. Or try to resist the temptation by taking deep breaths, or thinking of something else.

After all, why do we yearn to satisfy our cravings and gorge on sweets? Is it because we're that hungry, or do we simply want to fill the world with a bit of sweetness? Doctors know that the sugar we eat acts as 'fuel' for our brains.

When we're stressed, our brain requires sugar to calm us down. And that explains our craving for sweets!

So, if a harmless thing like pastries provides comfort, why should we resist it? As long as you only have one, there's no harm done.

How do rainbows form?

A long time ago, a rainbow was thought to be a bridge linking earth and heaven, the home of the gods.

Nowadays, we know that a rainbow is a physical phenomenon that occurs when it's raining while the sun is shining.

At first glance, sunlight appears white. But in reality, the colour white doesn't exist in nature! Sunlight is actually composed of different colours: red, orange, yellow, green, blue, indigo and violet.

When a ray of sunlight shines through a raindrop, it is refracted, and the light splits into a multitude of colours.

Because the water droplets are round, they each project a circular halo of colour, making the arched shape we know so well. The sunlight emerging from millions of raindrops creates a rainbow.

So are rainbows as round and circular as a drop of water? Well, yes, but from where we're standing, we can only see half of the circle. To see the rainbow in its entirety, you'd have to be in an airplane.

How do we evolve?

What's funny about evolution is that it actually evolves! Everything changes with time! Scientists have noted that from Big Bang (the great cosmic explosion that gave rise to the universe, some 10 or 20 billion years ago) through the emergence of human beings, evolution has become increasingly complex.

First there were the first particles of matter that made up the universe, followed by atoms and molecules – the first living cells.

Evolution progressed from organisms made up of one cell (unicellular) to the appearance of man, an organism composed of thousands of cells (multi-cellular), and possessing a highly-developed and complex brain.

40,000 years ago: 'Gotta go hunt!'

Today: 'Gotta go to work!'

But since the emergence of the Cro-Magnon man, who first appeared some 40,000 years, the human body has evolved little over the years. The morphology of the human species has remained virtually unchanged.

From that moment on, human evolution was marked by the acquisition of skills and experience, which allowed humans to perfect their knowledge in everything from the mastery of fire to the discovery of new planets. In addition to skills and knowledge, humans have also acquired freedom. We're willing to bet that humanity, unless it's bent on destroying itself, has plenty of good days ahead!

How can I tell my parents that I get scared when they yell at me?

Screaming at another person – whether it's justified or not – is an aggressive act which doesn't resolve anything. It doesn't make you right, and it doesn't lend authority.

Parents sometimes yell at their children because they fear their children are in danger. Because they're already burdened with problems related to work, money and health, parents remain on edge, and their anxiety manifests itself through screaming.

Once this stress is relieved, everything goes back to normal, like the calm after a big storm. But even if you understand the reasons for it, their outbreaks can still cause emotional pain.

No matter what their reasons are for yelling, it's important that you tell your parents how you feel about it, so that it doesn't become a habit. They will certainly take your request to heart.

However, if you can't get through to them and their yelling bothers you to such a point that it becomes a form of daily abuse, don't hesitate to seek help outside your family!

Ow!

How can we help poor people?

You tell yourself that it's impossible to ignore everything that happens in the world – or even in your own community or neighbourhood. Sometimes you feel the urge to roll up your sleeves and do something, rather than turn a blind eye to other people's problems.

But you may not always know how to help people without hurting or judging them. It's not easy. In addition to the logistical problems of shelter, food and work, hope is often what is most lacking in the lives of the poor.

The first step towards helping the poor live better lives is to change our perception of them. By doing so, you'll soon begin to think of spontaneous ways of helping them and how to best go about it.

The most important thing to remember is to treat others the way you would like to be treated in return: with respect.

How do broken bones heal?

Our skeleton – the sturdy framework that holds us together and gets us around – consists of no fewer than 206 different bones. Be they short, long or flat, our bones are covered by a bone tissue composed of the nutrients and minerals that makes them strong.

Throughout our lives, our bone tissue undergoes continual breakdown in order to release calcium into our bloodstream, and then rebuilds itself.

Sometimes, one or more of our bones may break due to a bad fall or an accident. By looking at an X-ray of the injured area, a doctor can determine the extent of the damage and how best to treat it. More often than not, the fracture will be clean. It will usually heal completely if it is kept in a cast or splint for several weeks.

But if the bone is displaced or chipped, plates and screws must be surgically implanted before it can be set in a cast.

Of course, it isn't the cast itself that heals the bone. The cast helps diminish the pain involved in moving the arm or leg around, so it can heal faster. When the injury is immobilised, the process of bone tissue restoration can begin. The new tissue is what seals the broken bone back together, like glue.

How can I admit that I don't like football?

Many children in your class wear a football shirt emblazoned with the name and number of their favourite player. This conveys their love of the game and, how, one day, they want to be the next football star, just like some children dream of becoming a world-famous singer.

Football sucks!

But what if neither of these things appeals to you? Does that mean there's something wrong with you? That you're abnormal? Crazy? Don't we maintain the right to our own tastes?

Of course! But you shouldn't go around criticising others because they don't like the same things as you. Claiming your superiority over others and making fun of their tastes is tantamount to excluding them, and thereby excluding yourself.

It's important to be open-minded and tolerant of a wide range of tastes and opinions. But it's not always easy.

If you don't like the same things as others, try to tell them gently, without sarcasm, that you have a preference for other activities. You might even pique their interest.

That said, the fact that you don't share a passion for football or music stardom with your friends doesn't mean that you don't have anything in common with them. There are still plenty of other things you agree on. Luckily, sharing interests isn't the only way of getting along with others!

How do migrating birds keep from getting lost?

Each spring, swallows start a new family. But did you know that they always return to the same nest they constructed the year before? Not their cousin's, nor their neighbour's. Their own!

There are more than 9,000 known species of birds; of these half thereof migrate when the seasons change, to hunt for food. Obviously, this practice didn't begin yesterday! As a result of numerous observations, scientists speculate that the origin of migration goes back to the ice age.

'Ready, here we go! Southward!'...

'This way!'

'No, it's the other way!'

'No that way!'

More than 15,000 years ago, Europe was covered in a layer of ice, forcing all of its living beings southward. When the climate warmed up, birds retained the habit of migrating from Europe to Africa, and back again.

Scientists can't fully explain how migrating birds develop their sense of direction. However, it's possible that they use several different systems and types of information to orient themselves, together or alternately: for example, the position of the sun in the sky, or the stars.

Birds also use their visual memory, which, like a camera, can capture the topography of the areas they travel through. They remember the shapes of the landscape – the hills, plains and rivers. Their olfactory memory (the memory of odours) also helps them find their way around. Migratory birds make use of their internal compass to distinguish between variations in the earth's magnetic field.

The wheatear bird can cover nearly 34,000 kilometres a year between Alaska and South Africa without getting lost. Despite all we know about migratory birds, this ability remains shrouded in mystery...

How can I confess to bad behaviour?

A bucket of water is strategically placed above the classroom door. The teacher opens the door and ends up soaking wet! Furious, the teacher demands that the culprit identify him or herself, but the classroom remains silent. It's only a matter of time before a general punishment is enforced. What should you do?

If you are guilty of having committed this deplorable act, you should admit to it immediately, despite your fears, before others are wrongfully accused. And if several of you pulled the stunt, you should convince all the others to turn themselves in to the teacher as well.

If you know who the perpetrators are and refuse to identify them, then you're as guilty as they are and should be punished equally. But what if you were going to warn the teacher to go through a different door, but you were afraid to be taken for a tattletale?

Tattling shouldn't only be done to prevent danger or a serious crime. If you're a witness to, or victim of, a crime or violent act, then, by all means, don't hesitate to tell someone, such as your teacher.

'Who did that?'

'He did it!'

'Who?'

'um, I already told you.'

But telling on someone so you come out looking good or blaming your own mistake on another person is disrespectful, and simply wrong. Even if you're scared of being ridiculed, you should make it a habit of thinking before you act, weigh the circumstances of telling on someone, and make the right decision.

How was medicine discovered?

Humans first discovered the benefits of herbs and plants in their environment by chance: cloves were discovered to be a good remedy for toothache and poppy flowers were found to relieve pain...Of course, there have also been some unfortunate accidents: the first person to have tasted hemlock (an extremely poisonous plant from the parsley family that can result in death) didn't live to describe its effects!

The discovery of remedies for different ailments emerged from these first experiments, with varying degrees of success. For a long time, their recipes were only known and passed down by a chosen few, such as priests, druids, witches or healers.

Today, technological advances have allowed us to not only artificially reproduce what nature creates on its own, but to invent new chemical compositions that are even more effective and less costly. This is what we call 'synthetic chemistry.'

It wasn't until the 19th century, when enormous progress was made in chemistry, that various parts of plants, minerals, and even animals, were extracted and combined for beneficial effect.

Yet despite these scientific achievements, the majority of people from a number of countries in Asia, Africa and South America continue to use traditional remedies aimed at maintaining the body's defences to prevent illness. Wouldn't it be ideal to combine these two kinds of medicine? That way, you could maintain good overall hygiene to ward off illness, but also take medicine when illness does occur.

'I have a stomach-ache!'

'Well, at least you no longer have a headache!'

How can I obey orders?

'Don't do this! Don't do that!' Enough already! Parents, teachers and generals all have this way of giving orders – it's unbearable! So how can I learn to obey without gritting my teeth or rebelling? Well, there aren't dozens of different answers to this question. You simply have to understand why the orders are given in the first place!

The only time we can bow to authority is when it's respectable, in other words, when it's good for everyone. Therefore, we maintain the right to disobey anyone who is unjust. But be careful! This is not an invitation to systematically question everything asked of you!

Every society needs laws, and those laws must apply to everyone. Laws help maintain equality and respect for each individual. This is why the vast majority of us obey them without even thinking about it.

For example, teachers are appreciated not because they're big and strong, but because they're fair. A kind of unwritten contract exists with the students based on mutual respect, in which everyone benefits. If, on the contrary, the teacher is unfair and punishes the students for no apparent reason, this would be intolerable, and obeying him or her would be impossible.

However, history has shown us how tyrants and dictators imposed laws serving their own ambitions. This kind of rule is unacceptable, even if the people who lived under it seemed to have had no choice but to keep quiet and submit to it. It is this kind of abuse of power which inevitably leads to war and hate.

How did April Fool's Day come about?

There are many theories regarding the origin of April Fool's Day, but they all reach the same conclusion: April Fool's is a day filled with pranks and jokes!

Until 1563, Easter, a Christian holiday commemorating the resurrection of Christ, marked the beginning of the calendar year. This day was determined by the religious calendar. But in an attempt to impose his authority, King Charles IX decided to change things.

From his accession to the French throne in 1564, King Charles IX decided to move the beginning of the new year from April to January 1st. The people who clung to the old calendar system continued to exchange the gifts and money that normally occurred during the celebration of the new year. Easter happened to fall on April 1st that year.

Eventually, the exchange of gifts transformed into 'gag gifts', and ultimately, jokes.

One of the most popular pranks of the time involved offering people fake fish, as fish is traditionally eaten to mark the end of Lent, which occurs during this period.

So, next time you plan to play a devious prank on somebody for April Fool's Day, remember to thank King Charles IX!

How do we remember things?

Try to picture our brain as a gigantic network of nerve endings, almost like an electric circuit filled with wires. This network is made up of numerous nerve cells called neurons. Neurons are connected to one another through synapses.

'Who are you again?...'

'Oh, right, you're my daughter.'

'Silly me!'

Each time we learn something new, this information flows through our nervous system by way of synapses and neurons. When we repeat the same lesson ten different times, the information always takes the same route.

After the 100th time, the route between neurons and synapses has been covered so many times that we end up memorising the lesson by heart. It's stocked in our memory. But how long will it remain there?

The sound of a door slamming shut remains in our memory for only a few thousandths of a second. The memory of a person's face we cross on the street stays with us for about several seconds. If we don't make any effort to recall it, we simply forget it.

On the other hand, the words and gestures we've learned over the years, the faces and places we love and the most significant moments in our lives stay in our memory for a long time.

That's why brothers and sisters, even though they grow up under the same roof and share similar experiences, don't always have the same memories. People usually remember only those things that have marked them personally.

Thematic Index